Embrace the journey
within & find
your true self!
Best Wishes,
Tejal
Bhavini

JALVINICOACHING. COM

You Got This!

Are You Ready?

To Unleash Your Strength,
Power and Potential
to Change Your World.

TEJAL & BHAVINI SOLANKI

ISBN: 978-1-9991921-0-5 (paperback)
ISBN: 978-1-9991921-1-2 (ebook)

Published by: JC Publishers

For our parents,
thank you for being our biggest cheerleaders

CONTENTS

INTRODUCTION

GETTING STARTED

"This is the beginning to changing
your world. You Got This!"

—Tejal & Bhavini Solanki

We've worked in human services for over 15 years. When we started our journey in this field, we had naysayers who would tell us to get a "real job" because a career that wasn't conventional (e.g., medicine, law, finance) was not considered a real job. During this time, we learned that following our passion and facing challenges without giving up is where our strength, power and potential lay to live our life.

Clients often come to us feeling stuck, spinning in the hamster wheel surrounded by doubts and toxic relationships and just unable to break free and speak their truth. They see themselves deserving more than just being stuck in a rut. Life doesn't have to be this way! By picking up this book you have decided to act and become the cause that creates a positive effect in your life. Are you ready to unleash your strength, power, and potential to change your world? The time is now to walk into your magnificence, to speak your truth and be heard, take on life with a fresh perspective, experience the power of tribe vibe, and thrive personally and professionally. Our role is to assist you to make powerful yet simple changes to discover your path, transform yourself and empower your life to achieve your life goals.

In the pages ahead you'll uncover how to create a basis to discover your limitless capabilities, experience changing your mindset and achieving success, and create an action plan to reach your potential and turn your life around. Your journey will be enhanced by the support from the You Got This! Tribe which is a powerful way to assist you in your success. Here you can share your experiences, access additional tools as well as templates, recommendations, and us. This is a private and safe space to share. We hope that you will get off the hamster wheel, learn from your challenges and celebrate your victories as you step outside your comfort zone into where the magic happens. You are awesome! YOU GOT THIS!

www.jalvinicreations.com/yougotthis
(Password: change-my-world)

CHAPTER 1

THE POWER OF YOUR MIND

"Your curiosity is your growth point always."

—Danielle LaPorte

Bhavini and I remember the time when we were on Prince Edward Island, Canada. We were standing on a rocky pathway feeling the bitterly cold wind blowing through our hair as we listened to the sounds of the waves crashing onto the rocks before us. It was peaceful, and we felt like we were in a trance. A short distance away, we could see majestic white icebergs, each one powerful and unique with its own characteristics—some were wide and rounded, others were uneven and reached almost 17 feet high. Suddenly, we heard a thundering and ear-piercing shriek in the air.

Before continuing with our story, we'd like to tell you about the power of the mind. Do you want to feel inspired and unstoppable?

Do you want to change your habits and be more effective and see the power of your mind? Yes? Then let's get into it.

We could only see 10% of the iceberg above the waterline.[i] Now, imagine if the iceberg was your mind. That 10% would be considered the conscious mind. The conscious mind determines our thoughts, logic, words, and actions within our awareness. If we were to ask you what the sum of seven and three is, it's your conscious mind that you use to do the addition. The conscious mind also directs and guides us, sets outcomes, and decides directions. If you are thirsty, you will decide to get a drink now or later. Ninety percent of the iceberg is under the waterline and so is not visible; our 90% is known as the unconscious mind. The unconscious mind is a vessel for thoughts, feelings, emotions, resources, and choices that we are not consciously aware of. The unconscious mind is responsible for all automatic body functions, such as your heartbeat, breathing, digestion, even blinking.[ii] You were not consciously aware of your breathing until right now. The waterline separates what's above and below the surface; in the mind, it's called the critical faculty. The critical faculty is the part of the mind that evaluates and filters information. More on this later.

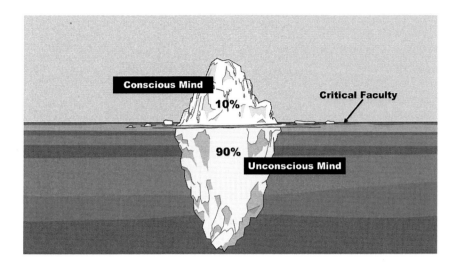

"The conscious mind determines the actions, the unconscious mind determines the reactions; and the reactions are just as important as the actions."

—E. Stanley Jones

Sigmund Freud, Carl Jung, and Milton Erickson were well-known psychologists who carved the way for us to understand the mind. Freud stated that the unconscious mind is the main source of human behavior,[iii] while Jung believed that the nature of the unconscious mind is a storage of repressed memories specific to the individual and our ancestral past.[iv] Erickson, on the other hand, deemed the unconscious mind to hold infinite wisdom that could be tapped into in order to solve issues.[v] The unconscious mind is emotional and irrational. It learns instantly and concurrently, whereas the conscious mind is the waking state of the mind and we spend most of our awake hours in this state. The conscious mind is about logic and reason. It also learns sequentially; that is, one thing after another, and it needs time to learn things. It also sorts and filters information because we can only retain a limited amount of data. As we mentioned before, the two-way barrier between the conscious and the unconscious mind is the critical faculty, which evaluates and filters information.

From birth, our mind is like a sponge and accepts and gathers everything positive or negative around us, from parents, teachers, religious leaders, and media, and this also includes the peripheral environment.[vi] This shapes whoever we think we are as an individual and how we see the world around us by the age of seven, when our critical faculty is developed. Everything negative or positive we felt, heard, and saw gets trapped under the critical faculty in the unconscious mind!

> *"We learn our belief systems as very little*
> *children, and then we move through life*
> *creating experiences to match our beliefs. Look*
> *back in your own life and notice how often*
> *you have gone through the same experience."*
>
> —Louise L. Hay

Let's explore the unconscious mind and what it is set up to provide and do for us.

1.   It runs the body.

As we mentioned before, the unconscious mind runs all the automatic functions of the body, such as our breathing, digestion, heartbeat, and so on. Imagine if you had to think about breathing in and out …

in and out…you'd be thinking about breathing all the time; however, the unconscious mind runs the body from a blueprint and makes it possible for breathing to happen automatically.

2.   It preserves the body.

The highest intention of the unconscious mind is to maintain the wholeness of the body and preserve it. It helps the body heal, fight infections, fix any damage, and warn us of any danger. For example, if you stepped in front of an oncoming bicycle, your unconscious mind would make you jump out of the way, and you will be safe. In times of emergency, our unconscious mind will automatically take over and it will be as if we are on autopilot.

3.   It is a storage for everything that's not in the conscious mind.

The unconscious mind stores your memories, life experiences, belief system, skills, situations, and images.

4.   It is symbolic.

The unconscious mind creates, uses, and responds to symbols. No matter where you are in the world, when you see a stop sign you will automatically stop! Road signs use symbols because the information gets transmitted to the unconscious mind faster than words.

5.   It will repress memories with unresolved negative emotions.

The emphasis here is on *unresolved*. These negative emotions (e.g., anger, sadness, hurt, fear, or guilt) are bottled up until they are solved.

Did you know that anger is linked to fatal heart disease and sudden cardiac arrest?[vii]

6. It presents repressed memories for resolution.

Do you wake up suddenly between 2:30am and 3:30am because something is bothering you? The unconscious mind brings unresolved memories to the conscious to be solved. In the short term, the unconscious mind will repress the memories, as you may not be ready to solve them; however, in the long term, the unconscious mind will continue to present the memories so that they can be released because, in time, the negative repressed emotions will end up showing up as a physical illness.[viii]

7. It takes everything personally.

Be careful when evaluating others because your unconscious mind takes everything personally. If you tell someone, "You're stupid!" you are giving instructions to your unconscious mind that YOU are stupid. Trippy huh? When you see the magnificence in others, you will begin to see your magnificence as well.

8. It does not process the negative.

Let's go back to the last time you told someone, "Don't forget to…" and they forget what you asked them to do! To the unconscious mind, don't forget implies to *forget*. Next time simply say, "Remember to…" Whether you want someone to do something for you or

you have a mental dialogue with yourself, make sure you are telling your unconscious mind what you want and not what you don't want.

It's great to know what the conscious mind, the critical faculty, and the unconscious mind can do. You must be wondering how you can activate the unconscious mind in your day-to-day life!

Well, ALL CHANGE BEHAVIOUR AND LEARNING happens at the unconscious level!

The conscious mind is the goal setter, whereas the unconscious mind is the goal getter. If there is a conflict between the conscious and unconscious mind, the unconscious mind usually wins! For example, if your conscious goal is to make more money and you unconsciously don't believe you are worthy of making more money, chances are you are not going to make more money. One of the things we'd like to point out here is that your reality reflects your beliefs, and all you have to do is look at your life to find what you believe. Take a moment and think about how your unconscious mind is working for you.

These beliefs are stories that we play in our mind that are not true. You choose to want to move forward or hold on to the story. We have powerful tools to dig up and eliminate limiting beliefs. We can't go through them fully here; however, here are some steps to get you started.

Step 1. Tap into all the thoughts and feelings (limiting beliefs) you get in different situations that are holding you back and write them down on paper.

Step 2. Imagine and really step into the new belief. It could sound like this, "My financial challenges have taught me a valuable lesson and I'm fully prepared to handle them now!"

Step 3. Act as if your new belief is true. This will be out of the box and scary! If you have learned from your past financial challenges, what will you do differently?

If you would like to eliminate your limiting beliefs, you can contact us via our website for a complimentary discovery call.

Here's a simple exercise to demonstrate the power of the mind. Watch the power of the mind demonstration video on the website and then imagine what is described below. Each step of the way, pause, close your eyes, and make the images real in your mind, then open your eyes and continue. The more real you can make it, the better this works. Ready?

Imagine you are holding a yellow, juicy, ripe, ready-to-squeeze lemon. You can feel the texture of the skin against your fingers, and as you bring the lemon closer to you, you begin to catch a hint of the wonderful fresh zesty scent it has.
Imagine placing the lemon on a cutting board on the counter in front of you, and picture yourself picking up a knife and slicing the lemon in half. Watch as the blade cuts into the lemon, releasing a spray of juice into the air. The air is filled with the scent of fresh lemon.

Take a moment now, close your eyes and imagine the scene. Visualize the sliced lemon, remember the sound it made as the knife sliced through the thick skin and into the middle of the lemon, releasing the juice into the air, so vivid you can almost taste it. When you have seen that in your mind, open your eyes. Now, take the knife and make a second cut, creating a lemon wedge. Imagine picking up that lemon wedge and bringing it to your mouth and biting down. Feel the juice washing over your tongue. Notice the bitter, sweet, sour taste as the juice fills your mouth. Feel as you swallow the juice. Did you notice a sour taste in your mouth? Could you hear the knife slicing through the lemon on the chopping  board? Is your mouth watering? You will find that simply by imagining that process, your body starts to react. Although you know there is no lemon, your unconscious mind prepares and acts in the same way that it would if you were to bite down on a lemon wedge.

Remember when we stood enjoying the powerful icebergs while we were on Prince Edward Island, and we heard a thundering and ear-piercing shriek in the air? Well right in front of us, a massive block of ice fractured and flipped over. It created small waves rippling off the shaking piece of ice and into the sea. We were able to see what lay beneath. The ice block underneath is something we'd never be able to assume without seeing it with our own eyes, just like the unconscious mind. The iceberg brought us to a clear realization: the power of the mind.

Join the You Got This! Tribe.

Share what you have learned in this chapter, what questions you have, and what we need to know.

www.jalvinicreations.com/yougotthis

Password: change-my-world

NOTES

_____

_____

_____

_____

_____

_____

_____

_____

_____

_____

_____

_____

_____

_____

_____

_____

_____

_____

_____

_____

_____

_____

_____

_____

_____

CHAPTER 2

LET GO OF THE INVISIBLE BAG OF ROCKS

*"When you let go, you create space for
better things to enter your life."*

—Anonymous

My friend Leya and I (Bhavini) were meeting up for dinner to catch up about her trip to South Africa. Leya was excited to see me, but as soon as I asked her about her trip the sparkle in her eyes disappeared with a big sigh! She told me that she had gone for her cousin Dina's, wedding. She hadn't seen Dina in 10 years and was looking forward to it. Leya's other cousin, Benisha from Toronto, was also attending the wedding. Leya thought the reunion would be amazing; however, a few days prior to the wedding, Dina was starting to show hostility toward Leya and her family. Leya then caught on that Benisha was creating the animosity within the family. The day of the wedding came and the tension within the families could be sliced through with a knife.

We'll come back to the story later. In the meantime, we will be looking at letting go, today! Do you want to take charge of you, experience a mind shift, and see yourself having healthy relationships? If you answered yes, then this chapter is for you.

We hold on to limiting decisions that we made, and negative emotions (anger, sadness, fear, hurt, guilt) like an invisible bag full of big heavy and small lighter rocks. We can choose to hold on to the invisible bag of rocks and complain and exhaust ourselves, or we can decide to drop it to experience the benefits of letting go.

Experts reveal that we have between 60,000 and 80,000 thoughts per day and that 80% of those thoughts are negative and 90% are repetitive.[ix] In Chapter 1, we talked about our unconscious mind being developed during infancy and continuing to develop from what we feel, hear, and see through our experiences as a child. At that point in time, our emotions and feelings become challenged and that's when we are most fragile. When we reach adulthood, we begin to focus on what we don't want rather than on what we want.

What we say to ourselves has an impact on what we do in our everyday life. The mind holds on with an endless set of expectations, beliefs and images that can get stuck in an unhealthy cycle. In the cycle, our mind goes down a dark path of creating a story about our self and it usually sounds like, "I'm not good enough," "I never have choices," "nobody loves me," or "no one cares for me." The more you think about it, the more the mind creates space to allow negative emotions to intensify; for instance, negative experiences early in life lead to negative emotions, like anger, which leads to acting out that anger toward other people, which causes other people to reject or get angry back, which reinforces the feelings of not being good enough, not being loved, and so on. These negative emotions need to be redirected and changed instantly so that you can focus your thoughts on what you want easily and effortlessly. There is no right or wrong time to let go; wherever you are in your journey, when the time is right for you to let go, that is the perfect time.

Here are three ways to let go.

1.　Getting it all out.

For thousands of years it has been recognized that anger contributes to several physical illnesses, especially heart disease.[x] Consistent fear is another negative emotion that can lead to excessive stress. One of the natural reactions that can cause anger stems from the irrational fear of something. Negative emotions are not safe or healthy for you. It is important to identify what upsets your feelings or emotions and to address the problem at the root cause.

Journaling is a way to get your feelings, thoughts, and emotions out. Instead of going over what happened, take a different approach, examine why that feeling showed up, and next time how would you react differently. More on journaling in a later chapter. Other ways would be to speak to a family member, friend, or therapist. Family and friends are great to have conscious conversations with; however, due to their biased support and they are unable to tap into the unconscious mind to release those old stories you keep playing over and over in your mind.

As Master Results Coaches, we work with the unconscious mind and will support you throughout your journey, you can contact us via the website for your complimentary discovery call.

Someone did you wrong! It hurts! The pain runs deep inside of you. What's worse is that you didn't deserve it. It wasn't your fault. Yet, every day you keep playing that painful movie in your head. Forgiveness is not about changing the past it's about changing the future. Forgiveness is a decision you make! Forgiveness is not about the other person. We have to forgive others who have hurt us because it is about breaking free from the pain that we have been holding on to like the invisible bag full of heavy rocks that serves no purpose in our life.[xi]

*"The truth is, unless you let go, unless
you forgive yourself, unless you forgive the
situation, unless you realize that the situation
is over, you cannot move forward."*

—Steve Maraboli

When you learn to forgive yourself, you are walking free, being the bigger person, taking the positive learnings and moving forward to being happy, healthy and at peace. This can be done by writing down your learnings from the situation and the benefits of forgiving the other person and yourself.

2.   Change your story, change your life.

When you are unable to let go, the negative limiting decisions from the past and negative emotions become part of your "story" and they sabotage your moving forward. Your story is what you tell yourself and others to justify your decisions and negative emotions. Allow yourself to open up, and feel the feelings, and to use the experiences in the journey, both good and bad, easy and hard, as learning tools. Life is full of teachers and lessons. Sometimes you will be the teacher and other times you will be the student learning the hard lessons.

A client walked into our office and started with, "Urgh! I stubbed my toe in the morning, and I was late to catch my bus and it's just been a terrible day." When he was done, I, Tejal, reminded him it was only 9am and he could decide to hold on to his story or change it to "I will have an amazing day!" He decided to have an amazing day. After our session he was attending an event and he emailed me later that day to inform me he'd won a prize and it was the first time he'd won something! By changing your story, you will learn to experience what is good for you more fully, as that is how you move forward and do better, live better, and choose better.

Letting go is choosing to drop the invisible bag of rocks and no longer dwell on things that are out of your control and instead focus on what you can control. From time to time you may pick up pebbles along the way and embrace the present and all it has to offer:

a new opportunity to begin again. No matter how many pebbles you pick up and how much you stumble on this journey of letting go, the present is always here to remind you that you don't have to stay stuck in yesterday or worry about what will happen tomorrow. Ultimately, you will drop the pebbles before they become an invisible bag of heavy rocks.

"The time is now, go ahead and shift your mindset and notice the small miracles you didn't before!"

—Tejal & Bhavini Solanki

You have been reading about letting go. You can feel yourself wanting to let go, and you might be wondering how you will experience letting go. Below are the instructions for a simple exercise you can follow and share. The only equipment you will need is a stress ball.

Step 1. Think of a limiting decision or negative emotion.

Step 2. Tighten your grip of the stress ball.

Step 3. Tighten the grip until it starts to feel uncomfortable, yet familiar.

Step 4. Open your hand and let the stress ball roll on the palm and fingers. Notice that you are holding onto it—it's not attached to your hand. We hold onto our emotions and then forget that we are holding on to them! It's even in our language; when we feel angry or sad, we don't usually say, "I feel angry" or "I feel sad," we say, "I am angry" or "I am sad." Without realizing it, we are misidentifying what we are experiencing. Oftentimes, we even believe a feeling is holding on to us.

This is not true; we are always in control and just not aware of it.

Step 5. Now, let go of the stress ball; simply decide to drop it. What happened? You let go of it, and it dropped to the floor. You may also notice your arm starts to relax and feel lighter. Was that difficult? No, it was a simple choice to decide to let go and release any limiting decisions and negative emotions.

Remember my friend, Leya? Well, Tejal became her coach, and weeks later she called me to say she had gone to a family event. As everyone stood in the buffet line, Benisha was standing in front of her, and when Benisha realized Leya was behind her, Benisha left the line. Leya found it strange, but said she no longer felt anger in Benisha's presence. She felt neutral and calm. Leya is now able to focus on the present and change her future by letting go, forgiving, and standing in her own power.

Join the You Got This! Tribe.

Share your aha moment from this chapter, what questions you have, and what we need to know.

www.jalvinicreations.com/yougotthis

Password: change-my-world

NOTES

CHAPTER 3

SNEAKY VILLAIN

*"A mind that is stretched by a new experience
can never go back to its old dimensions."*

—Oliver Wendell Holmes, JR

A grandmother was telling her grandson a story about life. She explains to him there are two wolves that live inside of us and they get into a battle with each other. One wolf is angry, sad, hurt, lives in fear and is guilty and has a scarcity mindset. This wolf sees the world as negative and unpleasant in every way. This wolf believes the world is a cold place and that people are up to no good. The other wolf is full of empathy, love, compassion, kindness, ambition, and power. The boy eagerly asks his grandmother, "Which wolf wins the battle?"

Before we tell you who wins, we should get on with the chapter! In this chapter, you will learn about the sneaky villain. Do you want to turn your life around by stepping out of your comfort zone, transforming yourself, and seeing the magic happen?

We all have our own sneaky villain that keeps us in our comfort zone, takes psychological, emotional and behavioral forms, and defines the routines of our daily life. If all you do is stay wrapped up in your cocoon like a caterpillar, keeping warm and cozy, then you will miss out on opportunities, new experiences, challenges, and being the magnificent butterfly. As you move toward transitioning, up levelling, and transforming yourself, you will feel a little or a lot of discomfort as you move toward the unknown where the magic happens.

In 1908, psychologists Robert M. Yerkes and John D. Dodson explained that a state of relative comfort creates a steady level of performance. Getting outside your comfort zone means doing things that are unfamiliar, maybe a little stressful, with the right amount of pressure. It also means keeping an open mind and exposing yourself to new experiences or accomplishing something with amazing results.[xii]

In Chapter 1 we talked about the critical faculty and the fact that from birth to seven years old, our mind is a sponge that accepts and gathers everything negative and positive around us from parents, teachers, media, and anyone it respects. By age seven, our critical faculty develops, and everything negative we felt, heard, and saw gets trapped as the sneaky villain in the unconscious mind. We all have the sneaky villain inside of us and it may show up as different things.

1. Sneaky Villain—Inner shitty committee.

One of the ways it shows up is as our inner shitty committee that says, "You don't deserve that," "It's too hard," "People won't like you," "You're not worth it." It stops you from living your happy, healthy, and successful life. To silence your inner shitty committee, you would have to identify what you feel, whose voice you hear, and what images you see when you hear the inner shitty committee's remarks so that you can clear them out to boost your confidence. This inner shitty committee hides in the unconscious mind and plays these remarks every day without you realizing they exist. You may find yourself spinning very fast, working very quickly, and running harder in the hamster wheel; however, you haven't been able to get to the next level of your life. You now want to expose and shut down the inner shitty committee once and for all. The good news is that as Master Results Coaches we can help you! Contact us through our website for your complimentary discovery call.

2. Sneaky Villain—Your negative thoughts.

The other sneaky villain, negative thoughts, comes from external influencers, such as the news, which we get at a dangerous rate through our social media accounts, TV, and apps. In the previous chapter, we explained that we have 60,000 to 80,000 thoughts per day, and 80% of those thoughts are negative and 90% are repetitive, which means we are carrying those thoughts into the next day. The external influencers strengthen the negative thoughts that get trapped in the unconscious mind because the unconscious mind takes everything personally. Thoughts like, "I avoid big crowded events because you never know…," "Do I deserve love when people around me are getting divorced?" "Why do I think I can lose weight?" Watch the news to be an informed citizen so that you are aware of what's going on in your neighborhood, province and country, and in the world. It is recommended that you limit your news consumption to one block of time each day, either afternoon or before dinner. Watching or reading the news before bed is a bad idea!

3. Sneaky Villain—Negative words.

How you and other people use negative words and how these words are attached to emotions is one of the sneaky villains. If someone calls you fat, a loser, stupid or useless, it hurts. When we attach emotions to every one of those words, we start to feel anger, sadness, fear, hurt, guilt, shame and rage. It's worse when we internalize these negative words because eventually our self-esteem and confidence decrease, our self-doubt increases, and our view of the world becomes negative. Let's switch the effects of the negative words and make them powerful words that we say to ourselves. One of the ways to flip these negative words to positive words is to write down the words that trigger emotions within you. For example, the word loser: when it shows up as a thought, write down the emotions associated with it such as loneliness, anger, sadness, and so on. When you find yourself saying, "I am a loser," you must stop yourself and say, "STOP! I can achieve this. I may need to create small goals and I may need a teacher, mentor, or coach to help me." By replacing the negative words with positive words, you will destroy the sneaky villain of negative words and you will awaken and engage your inner champion!

4. Sneaky Villain—Who are you spending most of your time with?

Take a moment to scan who you are spending most of your time with, do they charge your energy or drain it? Energy chargers will give you a sudden burst of energy and you will start to feel amazing. Energy drainers, on the other hand, will have a negative approach to everything. Some days may not be the greatest days for people and that's OK! However, not having a great day every day and not doing anything about changing that cycle makes that person an energy drainer. You want to surround yourself with energy chargers and people who have the same mindset. You want to start creating or joining a new tribe. For example, if you want to be successful, and success could mean getting the job of your dreams, finishing school or starting your own business, you want to surround yourself with people who have gone through similar struggles and have succeeded. These people are also continuously learning and growing. You can come across these people by joining meetup groups, reading books, listening to podcasts, attending seminars or getting a coach. Now, we are not saying that you have to remove these energy drainers out of your life; however, as you evolve and change yourself, they will automatically be left at the curb. All these sneaky villains keep you in your comfort zone. Stepping out of your comfort zone is to grasp new ideas and to be a little stressed with the right amount of pressure to push you into the magic. Here are a few exercises to get you out of your comfort zone.

Small steps.

You have a large goal to reach and it seems impossible to accomplish. Breaking down the large goal into smaller steps will shut down the sneaky villains and decrease your anxiety, and you will be more successful at steadily pushing through the boundaries of your comfort zone as you work toward reaching your bigger goal. In a later chapter we will look in depth at setting goals.

Modify your routine.

Following the same routine and listening to your inner shitty committee will give you the same results, keeping you in the hamster wheel. Some of the ways you can do things differently are taking a different route to work or school, taking the stairs instead of the elevator, taking dancing lessons or a wood-working class, making an easy recipe instead of ordering out, learning to play an instrument or complimenting one person each day. Like the old saying goes, "Insanity is doing the same thing over and over again and expecting different results." Therefore, alter your habits to see yourself getting closer to being happy, healthy, and successful.

Change your body posture.

Amy Cuddy,[xiii] a Harvard Business School professor, conducted a study on the benefits of power posing, and the technique is simple. Stand tall with your hands on your hips, feet slightly apart, shoulders back, chest out (picture your favorite superhero character stance). We love to add the following affirmations and say them out loud: "I am brave, I am fearless, I am bold, I am strong." Do this for two minutes in the morning (in your bedroom), before a meeting, before an interview (in your office or cubicle or bathroom stall), before attending a social event or any time you need to boost your confidence. In this stance and saying the affirmations out loud, you envision yourself achieving what you want which reprograms your disempowering thoughts and gets you to move forward.

Remember the grandmother who was telling her grandson about the two wolves inside of us? The grandmother replied, "Both wolves can come out powerful depending on which one you feed."

You can choose what external influencers you allow to have power over you, what words you use, who you hang out with, and whether you want to live a life of happiness, optimal health and success.

Join the You Got This! Tribe.

Share what you will be doing differently, what questions you have, and what we need to know.

www.jalvinicreations.com/yougotthis

Password: change-my-world

NOTES

CHAPTER 4

BE GOOD TO YOURSELF! SELF-CARE = SELF-LOVE

"Loving yourself starts with liking yourself,
which starts with respecting yourself, which starts
with thinking of yourself in positive ways."

—Jerry Corsten

I, Bhavini, had just graduated from university and was searching for a job. A couple of months later, my aunt, Harnisha, in Calgary, informed us that her cancer had returned after five years of being cancer free, and she would have to start her chemotherapy treatment immediately. A family decision was made that since she lived on her own and I was not working at the time, I was to spend three months with her as her caregiver. The first few weeks were difficult as I learned that it wasn't the same as taking care of someone who had a common cold or flu. We had to figure out a cooking schedule as the smell of food would make her nauseous. Also, her diet was different as we would have to make sure her blood count was up before her next chemo session. We barely went out as we had to make sure her immune system was not compromised. Her close friends would visit and want to take me out. I would decline the offer as I felt guilty leaving my aunt at home. Weeks went by, and I started to notice that I was falling asleep minutes after we sat down to watch a TV show. I realized after a few days that I was suffering from compassion fatigue because all I was doing was taking care of my aunt and not myself. One day, I was in the basement and saw some scrap paper lying around and I decided to staple them together.

In this chapter, we will discuss being good to yourself (self-care). Do you want to connect, maintain, and see a healthy relationship with yourself? Yes? Then this chapter is for you. The concept of self-care dates back to the 1950s and has medical roots where patients were given physical independence to do simple tasks such as personal grooming and exercise which increased their self-worth.[xiv] Self-care is about setting the intention and taking action to take care of ourselves in the most basic way. Anybody can do this guilt free! If you have ever been on a plane when the flight attendant goes through the safety precautions in case of an emergency and the oxygen mask is unleashed, you are instructed to put the oxygen mask on yourself first before you assist your neighbour, including a child. It is important to put on your mask first because if you run out of oxygen, you will not be able to help anyone else with their oxygen mask. Self-care is becoming increasingly popular thanks to social media; at the time of writing this book, there were 23.3 million Instagram posts with the #selfcare.

In Chapter 1, we talked about the unconscious mind's highest intention, which is to maintain the wholeness of the body and preserve it. When we do not take care of ourselves, we tend to want to withdraw ourselves. We might gain weight or lose our appetite. In Chapter 2, we spoke about forgiving yourself, as forgiveness is not about the other person; it's about deciding to move forward to being happy and at peace. In Chapter 3, we looked at how we use words and their attachments to emotions. By replacing the negative words with positive words, we awaken and engage the inner champion.

It's very important to make sure you take good care of your body, mind, and soul every day, not just when you get sick. Most of us are crazy busy, have stressful jobs or are too consumed with technology to make time for ourselves. We feel guilty about taking the time required to take care of ourselves. Self-care is usually last on the agenda and getting started can be quite the challenge. Here are 12 ways to get started with your self-care.

1.   Get some sleep!

Sleep can have a huge effect on how you feel both emotionally and physically. According to Statistics Canada, in 2017, it was recommended that adults aged 18 to 64 have 7 to 9 hours of sleep per night and seniors aged 65 or older get 7 to 8 hours of sleep per night.[xv] Not getting enough sleep can even cause major health issues.

Start by thinking about your nightly routine. A few ways to unwind would be breathing exercises, stretching, or visualization. Caffeine and alcohol should be avoided for most people at least five hours before bed. Alcohol is only a temporary sedative and once it's in your system it stimulates the brain causing sleep problems later at night.[xvi] One of the best ways to get good REM sleep is to limit electronics and keep the room quiet and dark.

2. Don't eat kale if you don't like it!

Yes, kale salads are the trend on social media of "wellness"— if you prefer spinach (or a plate of sweet potato fries) that's okay too.

 It's important to acknowledge that everyone is different in order to find the healthy sweet spot that works for you. Some of the most amazing self-care foods include avocado, fatty fish, blueberries, coconut oil, eggs, turmeric, walnuts, green leafy veggies, and broccoli. Every morning we make a cold-pressed greens juice that has celery, cucumber, green apple, ginger, cilantro and lemon. This juice has various benefits and one of the most important ones is that it increases our immunity through flushing our body with good bacteria that suppresses the bad bacteria.[xvii] It tastes delicious! Go ahead and make some for yourself. Having a healthy gut can have a significant impact on your overall health and well-being. What you eat impacts the bacteria that live in your stomach. A happy gut can lead to a happy person and vice versa.

3. Meditation.

Meditation is a technique used to increase state of mental awareness and focused attention. Meditation uses simple processes such as following your breath, repeating a mantra, or letting go of your thoughts. There are different forms of meditation that can be grouped into two main types. Mindfulness meditation involves being aware and involved in the present moment, concentrative meditation involves focusing our attention on a specific object while tuning out everything else around us. Scientists have shown that mindfulness meditation is the key element for stress reduction and overall well-being.[xviii] If you have never meditated, you can start with focusing on your breath or repeating a word such as "OM" or an affirmation such as "I am relaxed" for

3 minutes and increase your time to 20 minutes. Visit our website to practice mindfulness meditation.

4. Exercise daily as part of your self-care routine.

Exercising daily for 20 to 30 minutes will help you both physically and mentally by improving your mood, reducing stress, and possibly losing weight. Research shows that minimal exercise is better than none, so even starting with walking around the block (with a friend

or a dog) a few times can increase your heart rate and get you moving! Other exercises that may fit into your schedule more easily would be biking, jogging, or yoga.[xix] Creating a routine that works for you is essential.

5.   Say no to others and say yes to your self-care.

In the past, we would struggle and take on a lot of tasks, not being able to say no to friends and family. If they wanted something from us, we would say yes, and we would do it. Later, we would feel overwhelmed and stressed, and we know that there are a lot of people out there that feel overwhelmed, stressed, and overworked because they are unable to set boundaries. Here's a secret: no is a complete sentence. To be polite you can say, "No, thank you." If you need to buy some time you can say, "Let me get back to you." This is when you check if you have the time and energy to give. When you do get back you can either say, "Yes," or give your conditions, "I will be able to help you after I..." or you could just say, "I can't this time around." Note that there is a difference between refusal and rejection. You are not rejecting the person you are just turning down the request. It took us a little practice to politely say no, and when you learn to say no, you will start to feel more empowered and have more time for your self-care.

6. Take a self-care trip.

Whether you are working, job searching, helping others with tasks, or taking care of a loved one (if you can get respite care for the day), or even if you just need a break, a day trip to a nearby town or waterfront, or a hike, or a spa day can help you disconnect, relax, and rejuvenate. The purpose is to get away from your normal schedule and just do something for yourself.

7. Spend time outside.

Whether you are sitting in your backyard, walking in the park or being in nature, spending time outside will help you reduce stress

and be more mindful and will help boost your immune system. Research shows that spending time outside can boost your energy, overcome symptoms of depression or burnout and help you get a good night's sleep.[xx]

8. Get organized.

Having a planner or calendar with all your responsibilities and appointments will allow you to figure out exactly what you need to do to take better care of yourself.

9. **Schedule your self-care time, and guard that time with everything you have.**

Block 20 minutes to an hour to yourself every day on your calendar. If you have kids, you can split the time during the day when you have somebody to help you with them. This habit will train you and everyone around you that this time is extremely important to you.

 Self-care time can be spent alone or shared with family or friends. Time alone will help you contemplate ways to move forward in life as well as keeping you grounded. Sharing your self-care time with friends will help you feel more connected and relaxed.

10. **Colouring for adults.**

Just like meditation, colouring relaxes the fear center of the brain and generates mindfulness. This convenient, creative, and therapeutic hobby diminishes negative thoughts, brings out the inner child, and allows us to be at peace with ourselves.[xxi] There are colouring books for just about everything these days. Find some coloured pencils or crayons and colour in the artwork on the next two pages.

11. Journaling.

Journaling is one of the best ways to relieve stress and process emotional issues and is essentially free and easy to do. Journaling will help you keep a positive mindset focused on your goals as well as being productive and happy. You do not need to wait for a new year or new season. You can journal right now! It takes 20 minutes. Here are some guidelines to journaling. Store your journal in its own special place so

that the temptation for others to read is diminished. Every entry needs to be dated. Dating the entry gives you a snapshot of where you are in life and keeps track of your progress. Next, give yourself permission to tell the truth, even if the truth seems too bright or too harsh. In addition, as you're going through the ups and downs of life, write down the learnings from that day. Lastly, gratitude is the vitamin for the soul, so go ahead shift your mindset and notice the small miracles that you didn't notice before. There are no rules, any way you do it is perfect! There is a free downloadable The Power of Journaling template and video on our website.

Self-Hypnosis for self-care.

efore we started our journey in becoming internationally recognized hypnotherapists and hypnotherapy instructors, we would use meditation as one of the ways for self-care for the mind. Hypnosis is a term that is often puzzling, misunderstood or convoluted. It is a trance-like state and, in reality, we all go in and out of mild "trances" every day. This happens when we focus attentively on something and block everything else out, or when we "zone out" either in front of the TV or with a book. Hypnosis is a wakeful state where you are in a deep state of relaxation and are hyper focused. In this heightened state of mind, hypnosis is used to make changes to your self-beliefs and enable you to make changes in your life using positive  suggestions. All hypnosis is self-hypnosis. Hypnosis can improve the quality of sleep. It is one of the best ways to reduce stress, anger and anxiety, to boost confidence and to lead to a deep relaxing experience that brings about positive, profound and lasting changes. We use self-hypnosis and meditation twice a day. If you want first-hand experience of hypnosis, watch our video on our website. If you want to be trained in hypnosis, we offer certification and board-designation trainings in hypnosis. Contact us via our website for details.

The key to living a balanced life is to find your own rhythm and routine. Self-care has to be an active plan that can be done alone or as a community, as you will increase your commitment to it. Lastly, be aware of what you do, why you do it, how it feels, and what the outcomes are for your self-care. Remember, self-care is all about the relationship with yourself and others. If you are struggling to make self-care a priority, you can contact us for your complimentary discovery call via our website. There is a simple one-minute exercise on our website. You can use this as a quick mental break anytime during the day. If you would like to share this exercise with someone, all you have to do is read the script below in the same tone and tempo as in the video.

Get comfortable and breathe in 1, 2, 3…breathe out 1, 2, 3.

Take a moment to scan through your body and see what wants to relax and let go a little.

Take a full, deep breath in, filling the chest, filling the lungs, and slow out breath, feeling the sensations of the breath as you release.

And again, breathe in and breathe out, letting your breath resume its natural rhythm.

Open your senses and relax with the background of life.

Breathe in 1, 2, 3…breathe out 1, 2, 3, and come back to the room. Welcome back!

Remember when I, Bhavini, was suffering from compassion fatigue and saw some scrap paper lying around in the basement? Well I stapled them together and on the top sheet I wrote "BHAVINI'S JOURNAL." While my aunt would be resting, I used that time to write about my experience in Calgary and what I was learning about myself. I would also take some time to meditate (this was before I learned self-hypnosis). By taking care of myself I noticed my aunt's perception and mindset started to shift during her treatment. Soon, we were able to go out with her friends for breakfast, lunches, and dinners, take a spontaneous trip to Canmore, a tiny town, to have hot chocolate, and take her dog, Shaka, for a brisk walk around the block.

*"Take care of yourself so you
can take care of others."*

—Diane C.

Join the You Got This! Tribe.
Share what you will be doing differently, what questions you have, and what we need to know.
www.jalvinicreations.com/yougotthis
Password: change-my-world

NOTES

CHAPTER 5

MAKING SENSE OF THE WORLD THROUGH LANGUAGE

*"To effectively communicate, we must realize
that we are all different in the way we perceive
the world and use this understanding as a
guide to our communication with others."*

—Tony Robbins

Kalina was a good girl, she was very quiet and kept to herself. She was a girl of few words only because she was shy and sometimes felt she had nothing interesting to share. That changed when Kalina and her family had to move. As she was exploring her new house, she discovered a huge attic full of old treasures. She came across a big chest containing all sorts of things. As she lifted all the things out one by one, an enchanted book floated out of the chest. Kalina didn't see anything holding it up. She took the book to her room and quickly hid it and put her puppy, Snowy, on guard duty over it. That night, when her parents were asleep, she sat with Snowy and started reading the book. It was a storybook, and as she read,

Snowy started speaking to her. "What an interesting book you've found! It seems to have some exciting stories!" Kalina couldn't believe her ears. Snowy continued talking, telling her things, and asking a lot of questions. Kalina sat up straight and asked, "You can talk?" "I guess so," answered Snowy. "Instead of just thinking things, now I'm saying them too. It hasn't changed much for me; I guess it was the book that did it, though." Kalina decided to test the book with her other pets. One after another, her cat, Ginger and her fish, Fishy, all started chatting with her and telling her some interesting stories about themselves, their day, and their lives. Kalina was thrilled to hear all the stories and continued to chat with her friends for the next few days. One day, mysteriously, the book disappeared. With it went the animals' voices. Kalina frantically searched for the book everywhere but couldn't find it.

In this chapter, you will learn to make sense of the world through language. Do you want to get a handle on, pay attention to, and get a perspective on, how we use our words to communicate? Yes? Then let's show you!

The most important skill to have in life is the art of communication. We have seen what happens when people haven't been able to get their message across clearly. You've had times where no matter how clear your message was, you know deep inside that you did not connect with the other person. You question yourself, "Is it something I said?" or "Did I not say something?" Maybe it's neither. Chances are you didn't understand how to communicate in the other person's unique and instinctive way of receiving the message. If you look around your current environment everything that you are seeing, hearing, touching, tasting, and smelling at this moment is an internal representation of your world. There are certain words that you choose to describe your situation. When you are able to make sense of the world through language you will become an effective communicator and save yourself hours of arguments and miscommunication.

"The single biggest problem in communication is the illusion that it has taken place."

—George Bernard Shaw

Richard Bandler and John Grinder are co-creators of Neuro-Linguistic Programming. They believe that each person has a preferred representational system in which they are able to create an experience (in their mind).[xxii] For example, someone whose preferred representational system is visual would be able to visualize things in either creating or recreating an experience.

In Chapter 1, we learned that the conscious mind determines our thoughts, logic, words, and actions within our awareness. One of the most important characteristics of the conscious mind is that it likes everything to make sense. You are currently using the conscious mind to read and process the words on this page. As you say the words on this page, in your mind you are making sense of the text and establishing how the meaning of the text relates to you. To make sense of the world through language, it is important to understand your preferred representational system and the one that the person you are communicating with uses, as only then will you be able to communicate in the most effective way. There are four main representational systems.

1. Visual (seeing)

People who are visuals prefer in-person interactions or video calling as they want to see the other person's reactions. Visuals are imaginative and may have difficulty putting their ideas in words. They are able to

see the bigger picture, want to see or be shown concepts or ideas, or how something is done. They speak faster than the general population. They are organized, neat, and well-groomed. Visual people often sit forward and upright in their chairs or stand straight with their eyes up and breathe from the top of their lungs. Visuals usually have a higher-pitched tonality. Here are some of the visually descriptive words commonly used: see, look, bright, and imagine. Visually descriptive phrases include take a closer look, and show me what you mean.

2. Auditory (hearing)

People who are auditory prefer to communicate through spoken language and need to be heard; thus, phone calls would be welcomed. The auditory person learns by listening and asking questions and enjoys discussions. They typically have conversations with themselves (some may even move their lips when talking to themselves). They are easily distracted by noise and usually like music. They memorize

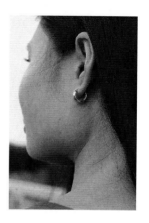

steps, procedures, and sequences. Auditory people are more aware of changes in the tone of people's voices and are more responsive to certain tones of voices or sets of words. Auditory people stand with their arms folded across their chest with the head tilted down and to the side, perhaps to listen, and they breathe from the middle of their chest. Descriptive words commonly used are hear, tell, sound, and listen, and phrases include I hear what you say, and sounds good.

3. Kinesthetic (feeling)

People who are kinesthetic prefer in-person interactions and tend to stand closer because they want to feel the other person's energy. They

respond to physical rewards and touch. They learn by doing, moving, or touching. They make decisions based on their feelings. Kinesthetics tend to dress and groom themselves more for comfort than how they look. Kinesthetics sit slightly bent forward with rounded shoulders as they speak and listen. They breathe from the bottom of their lungs, so you'll see their stomach go in and out when they breathe. They often move and talk very slowly. Kinesthetically descriptive words commonly used are grasp, feel, touch, and relaxed, and phrases include I have the feeling that, and I couldn't put my finger on it.

4. Auditory Digital (using language)

People who are auditory digital prefer to communicate using writing,

 such as emails, which will generally be long, detailed and filled with lots of data. In phone conversations with auditory digitals,

one must be prepared, precise, and task oriented. Small talk is irrelevant to them; thus, conversations will go straight to business. Auditory digital people learn by working things out in their mind as they like to analyze things and solve problems. Our father is an auditory digital because often he will say, "I told you about it," when he actually didn't tell us; however, he had the conversation with us in his mind! Auditory digitals tend to have a structured and deliberate walking pattern. They demonstrate few, if any, facial expressions and few body gestures and have a more formal and conservative look. Some auditory digital descriptive words include sense, experience, understand, and change, and phrases such as I know that, and I have to think about it are common. Once you familiarize yourself with your representational system and that of others you will be able to gain powerful insights into how subtle yet powerful this concept is because it is key in communicating and entering the other person's world of language.

Discover Your Preferred Representational System

To find out your representational system preference, complete the short assessment below.

Step One

Read each statement (in **bold print**) below. Rank each of the four answers that follow. Only use each number (1, 2, 3, 4) one time for each statement.

4 = most like you	3 = a lot like you
2 = a little like you	1 = not much like you

For example:

I make important decisions based on

    3 ●   gut level feelings.

    4 ■   which way sounds the best to me.

    2 ◆   what looks best to me.

    1 ★   a precise review and study of the issues.

1.   I make important decisions based on

— ● gut level feelings.

— ■ which way sounds the best to me.

— ◆ what looks best to me.

— ★ a precise review and study of the issues.

2.   During an argument, I am most likely to be influenced by

— ■ the other person's tone of voice.

— ◆ whether or not I can see the other person's argument.

— ★ the logic of the other person's argument.

— ● whether or not I feel I am in touch with other person's true feelings.

3.   I most easily communicate what is going on with me by

— ◆ the way I dress and look.

— ● the feelings I share.

— ★ the words I choose.

— ■ the tone of my voice.

4.   It is easiest for me to

— ■ find the ideal volume and tuning on a stereo system.

— ★ select the most intellectually relevant point concerning an interesting subject.

— ● select the most comfortable furniture.

— ◆ select rich, attractive color combinations.

5. (There is no question, just rate 1-4)
— ■ I am very attuned to the sounds of my surroundings.
— ★ I am very adept at making sense of new facts and data.
— ● I am very sensitive to the way articles of clothing feel on my body.
— ◆ I have a strong response to colors and to the way a room looks.

6. People really know me best when they
— ● experience what I am feeling.
— ◆ see my perspective.
— ■ listen carefully to what I have to say and how it is said.
— ★ are interested in the meaning of what I'm doing or saying.

7. I am more likely to
— ■ want understanding of the facts you tell me.
— ◆ picture the overview or plan.
— ★ sequence the information you give me to make sense of it all.
— ● get a handle on the feeling of the project.

8. Describing myself I'd say
— ◆ showing it to me makes it believable.
— ■ the sincere tone of your voice makes it believable.
— ● when it feels right it's believable.
— ★ when it makes sense it's believable.

9.   In times of stress I'm most challenged with

— ★ trusting the people or situation.

— ■ being diplomatic.

— ● separating what my feelings are from what other people are feeling.

— ♦ being flexible and changing plans easily.

10.   (There is no question, just rate 1-4)

— ★ I easily receive inner inspirations.

— ■ I can tell easily where new ideas fit.

— ● I easily follow the direction of the tried and true methods.

— ♦ I easily organize and plan the timing of things.

Step Two

Copy the ranks from your answers into the boxes below. In all 10 sections your answers were preceded by ●, ■, ♦, ★. Put '●' answer in the column headed ●, and the ■ answers in the ■ column. Then add up the numbers in each column.

The maximum column score is 40 and the minimum is 10.

T	●	■	♦	★
For example	*3*	*4*	*2*	*1*
1				
2				
3				
4				
5				
6				
7				
8				
9				
10				
Totals				

Step Three

Copy the total score from the columns above and match the columns ●, ■, ♦, ★ with ●, ■, ♦, ★ below to give you your score results.

Score results:

— ● Visual

— ■ Kinesthetic

— ♦ Auditory

— ★ Auditory Digital

The comparison of the totals gives the relative preference for each of the four representational systems.

Your exercise for the next 21 days is to pick a family member or close friend in your life and listen to the types of words they use. You will notice they will probably use all four representational systems; however, they will have one preferred representational system. Then practice translating your language to their representational system. If they say, "I don't **see** your point," don't say, "Let me repeat it," instead say, "Let me **show** you what I mean." If they say, "What you're suggesting doesn't **feel** right to me," don't say, "Take a different view," instead say, "Let's **touch** upon the points another way." If they say, "I've **tuned** you out," don't say, "You're insensitive," instead say, "Let's **talk** it over." If they say, "You make **no sense**," don't say, "You don't see what I mean?" instead say, "Let me give you **more details**." Practice with other people you know and listen to conversations on the radio or TV to develop your skills. Eventually you will find yourself doing it automatically. Become aware of how other people think, become flexible in how you respond, and develop excellent communication skills.

Remember, the little girl Kalina, who couldn't find her enchanted floating book anywhere? Well, she was starting to miss her chats with her animal friends. She remembered how interesting the animals' stories were and realized that she hardly spoke to the other children in her class and they probably had interesting stories to tell too! Kalina made an effort to start talking more to the other children in her class and school. Kalina learned to understand her own and other people's representational systems through her conversations with the animals. For instance, Snowy said he was always thinking things and now could say them; Kalina learned that she had lots to say and that others would listen. At the end of the school year, Kalina had entered their world of language and she had more friends than she had when she first started school.

Join the You Got This! Tribe.

Share what you will be doing differently, what questions you have, and what we need to know.

www.jalvinicreations.com/yougotthis

Password: change-my-world

NOTES

CHAPTER 6

LIVE LIFE ON YOUR TERMS

"There is no greater agony than bearing an untold story inside you."

—Maya Angelou

In 2013, I, Tejal, developed a cough. I didn't think much of it at first, as I thought it was due to of lack of sleep. A couple of weeks went by and the cough disappeared. It reappeared three months later. It was subtle at first, and then it started to get out of control. My dry cough was so bad that I was unable to finish sentences without coughing through them. Oh the frustration! At work, I'd have a disclaimer so my clients would know I wasn't contagious, and it was not as bad as it sounded! I had gone to see my doctor and a few specialists, and no one was able to figure out the cause of my cough. It was shocking to be told that nothing was physically wrong when the symptoms felt and sounded severe. I had gone to see a naturopath and she found other minor health issues that I was able to resolve; however, the cough lingered. At one point, I lost my voice!

In this chapter, we will be looking at living life on your terms! Do you want to get a handle on your strength from within and experience speaking from your power? Are you ready to change your world?

Many people go through life feeling stuck, spinning in the hamster wheel carrying negative emotions from childhood into adulthood and are unable to break free. YET, they know they deserve more and want to get out of the rut! Anytime you find yourself at a crossroad of whether you should speak your truth or not, you will be able to use these easy ways to navigate that major turning point. You will be able to communicate authentically as it is important to share our true selves with others, including our feelings, needs, boundaries and desires. It's taken me many years to learn how to communicate in an assertive and authentic way. It felt like an unimaginable challenge to speak my truth, like climbing a mountain with an elephant on my back. I would always overcommit and give my word to get something done, whether it was to my family, friends, or coworkers. I would walk away from conflicts without saying a word and wish I'd spoken up for myself. In all my close relationships with people, I would be the one doing the majority of giving rather than receiving. Beneath all the layers of being a rescuer, people pleaser, telling white lies, and insecurities, I wanted to break free because I knew there was a bold, confident, powerful woman just like She-Ra: Princess of Power inside of me. (In the 80s, She-Ra was a superhero fictional character.)

On my own personal journey to becoming that woman, I had to learn that assertive authentic communication is like working a muscle—hard and exhausting at first, but getting better as I created a habit with exercise. Just as with all exercises, you don't walk out of your house and run a marathon! You first have to start slow: stretch, warm up, jog and run in your neighbourhood, and so on.

We feel totally in control when life is running smoothly and everything is going great! Life is such that there will always be negatives and positives. Our reactions, decisions, avoiding situations, and sabotaging our goals are all driven by emotions. Most of us don't understand our emotions or exercise much control over them. As we mentioned earlier, negative emotions such as anger, sadness, fear, hurt, and guilt can create a blockage in our brain; thus, we keep spinning in the hamster wheel and don't allow for a different sort of outcome in life such as seeing a boost in our confidence and self-esteem.

Let's say you agreed to do something or take on someone else's task and your inner voice wants to scream "NO!" as you feel a surge of anger. Anger is your body's reaction to denying your truth. Negative emotions can be very dangerous for you when suppressed, as the suppression can isolate you from others and it may show up as a physical illness as well.[xxiii] Let's warm up your assertive and authenticity muscles, and prepare you for a lifetime of speaking your truth!

1.   Naming the feeling, right now.

Go ahead, scan and reflect through your mind and body. Take a deep breath in. Does the air go all the way to your belly, or does it only reach your chest? Notice how it feels. Notice the strain you might be carrying in your neck and shoulders and notice how your heart is feeling. Perhaps this is the first time in hours that you have taken the time to scan and reflect. Many of us are so wired that we reach for our phones to disconnect and are even sometimes numb to feeling the feelings and to remembering that we have a body. To be able to communicate your feelings assertively and authentically, you first must know how you feel.

2.   When someone asks you how you are, tell them the truth.

When was the last time someone asked you how you were doing and instead of giving them the socially normal response of "I'm good" or "Fine, thanks," you actually said, "I feel like crap, but doing the best I can. Tomorrow's another day," or "I'm feeling awesome. It's been an exciting and inspiring day," or "I'm so stressed out my body feels numb."? Habitually you still answer with "I'm good," or "Fine, thanks" because the world would end if you shared your true feelings! Remember, being genuine in your responses when someone asks, "How are you?" can establish a real sense of closeness, understanding and trust. Give yourself permission to share what's going on with you. As you know, life has its valleys and mountains and we all deal with them. It's ok to show the vulnerable side of you, as it will allow you to receive the gift of compassion and empathy from others.

3.   The beauty of silence. You don't always need to respond.

Being a people pleaser, I would find silences in conversations eerie and I would jump in and would talk about anything to fill the space. Later, I'd wonder why I said anything! After the conversation I'd be emotionally drained. I have realized that silence is beautiful; silence allows for whatever you are talking about to sink in, you are present in the now and sometimes the most authentic response is to say nothing at all.

4.   Keep it simple.

There are two sides to being authentic and speaking your truth. As I've mentioned before, it means being vulnerable. You can be speaking your truth to create boundaries, to have difficult conversations, or to create distance from others, and speaking your truth will create trust, love, and bring people closer. We are sometimes afraid to be vulnerable, to bring people closer to us because we are afraid of what they might think of us. Well I have news for you, what other people think of you is none of your business! Being vulnerable causes us to give control of our emotional state to others and that could definitely affect us, sometimes deeply. Go ahead, keep it simple and today, now, tell someone who you haven't told that you truly care for them that you care for them and see what happens.

5.   Declare one thing you really want.

"A lot of people are afraid to say what they want. That's why they don't get what they want."

—Madonna

Just like you, there are many things I want. What we desire is a significant part of who we are. Oftentimes, circumstances mean we put the needs of others before our own and lose what we really desire. If you've been out of touch with your own desires for a long time, getting back in touch could be life changing. Wanting a new job or going back to school to study can be scary and radical. Give yourself permission to take some "self-care time" and reflect on what you truly want. Just notice how it feels, to really want the thing you want.

*"You know, when you're real and speak
your truth (in respectful ways), people won't
always like you. But you'll like you."*

—Robin Sharma

I get it. We live in the fast lane, overwhelmed with the stimuli from every direction while trying to catch up with life, which is exhausting because it feels like we're running on empty. In this state, we are in response mode and our inner self can't emerge as we are not thinking deeply and aren't present in the now at all.

Start with taking a 15-minute technology diet every day. This means no phone, no TV, no computer, no screen of any kind. Spend time outdoors, drink your tea or coffee outside on the balcony or backyard, watch your kids play, better yet play with them, read a book…give your mind the time to explore and see the magic of creativity and innovation take over. The following exercise will help get out of your shell. Keep it simple.

You miss somebody?

Call (Hi, I was thinking about you and I miss you. Or I was thinking about you and I miss how we used to chat for hours)

You want to meet up?

Invite (Hi, we haven't caught up in a while. Are you free for coffee sometime?)

You want to be understood?

Explain (I would like to clarify….)

73

You have questions?

Even if you think it's silly, ask (I've never watched Game of Thrones, what's it all about? For this one, be prepared for the shocked reaction that you haven't watched the show!)

You don't like or do like something?

Say it! (Give your feedback in this way, what I loved was…, what I'd like to see more of is…, overall this was…)

You want something?

Ask for it. (I'd like 15 minutes of me time every day when I get home as it will allow me time to reset my mind and be re-energized to be fully focused on us, our family, for the evening.)

You love or care for someone?

Tell them! (Hi, I wanted to let you know. I love you! Or I wanted to let you know that I care for you.)

Remember, when I had my cough and lost my voice? Well through my journey of transformation I learned that emotional stress can cause a cough and affect our voices and how this can be treated. As I went through my own personal breakthrough session, I was able to tap into the unconscious and release the suppressed negative emotions of anger, sadness, fear, hurt, and guilt and the attached memories. I got my voice back! Assertive and authentic communication has made my life much simpler. I work on this assertive and authentic muscle and the growing pains have truly enabled me to live in alignment with my inner truth and find freedom, self-respect, and confidence along the way. I am also able to speak clearly and confidently from my power just like She-Ra!

Join the You Got This! Tribe.

Share what you will be doing differently, what questions you have, and what we need to know.

www.jalvinicreations.com/yougotthis

Password: change-my-world

NOTES

CHAPTER 7

KEEP LEARNING

"Every next level of your life will demand a different you!"

—Leonardo Dicaprio

I, Tejal, came across a free two-day seminar which was not on my radar, but since I was available that weekend, I decided to sign up. I was also given the opportunity to bring a guest so I asked Bhavini if she would like to join me. She was slightly reluctant but decided to join me to see what it was all about. When we got to the venue there were approximately 200 people waiting to get in. We met people who were in various industries: DJ, teachers, psychologists, financial analysts, real estate agents, and many more. Off the bat, the presenter was energetic, funny, inspiring, and captivating! There were certain things he said that reinstalled our prior knowledge and we also learned new and effective ways to accomplish things. The seminar gave us a chance to network with the people in the room whereby we built new friendships and gained new ideas that left us inspired. Toward the end of the day, I turned to Bhavini and said,

"We are going to write a book!" Bhavini looked at me with shock and disbelief and said, "NO!"

In this chapter, we will look at ways to keep learning. Do you want to create a foundation to experience the power and secret of learning? Many people brag about how few books they have read since leaving formal education. One time, at work, I was looking at a training opportunity that we all received via email. A coworker was passing by my office and popped in to ask, "Are you going to that training?" I replied with excitement, "Yes!" She laughed and said, "You like to attend every training even though it's not related to the job description." For me there is nothing more exciting than learning something new, whether it's watching the show *How it's Made*, taking a course, attending a webinar, or learning from a friend. As soon as I am done, I am always thinking about whom I will share my new knowledge with, and how I will apply the information in my daily life. Assuming you already know enough is to be stagnant and you start declining. We live in an ever-changing world and you never are really finished learning anything completely. Some people emphasize being right rather than being successful.

"Anyone who stops learning is old,
whether at twenty or eighty. Anyone
who keeps learning stays young."

—Henry Ford

Researchers from University College London followed approximately 7,500 civil servants for more than 20 years and they found that those who reported high levels of boredom were more than twice as likely to die of heart disease.[xxiv] Who would have thought that you could actually be bored to death!

New learnings and experiences will increase your dopamine levels as well as improve your brain's neuroplasticity (the brain's ability to change). Dopamine is one of the feel-good chemicals our body releases to let us know we have done a good job. University of Washington's Eric Chudler Ph.D., explained, "Neuroplasticity describes how experiences reorganize neural pathways in the brain. Long lasting functional changes in the brain occur when we learn new things or memorize new information… To illustrate neuroplasticity…imagine making an impression of a coin in a lump of clay. In order for the impression of the coin to appear in the clay, changes must occur in the clay— the shape of the clay changes as the coin is pressed into the clay. Similarly, the neural circuitry in the brain must reorganize in response to experience or sensory stimulation."[xxv]

In Chapter 3, we talked about getting out of your comfort zone and as you move toward transitioning, up-levelling and transforming yourself, and as you move toward the unknown where the magic happens, you will feel a little or a lot of discomfort. Let's face it, we live in a competitive world, and employers are looking for value-added employees who are knowledgeable and skilled. Yes, most times employers expect you to keep learning to stay on top of your profession and that's great, but what about your own feeling of accomplishment and satisfaction when you've learned something new for yourself? Successful people are constantly learning, and they will seek and find people who know what they are talking about and will learn from them. You will also find that successful people spend a lot more time listening than speaking.

"Always walk through life as if you have
something new to learn and you will."

—Vernon Howard

Now, when I talk about success, I'm looking at success in whatever area(s) you'd like to achieve more—career, family, relationships, cooking, traveling, business, and health. Here are the five ways to keep learning.

1.   Read

Read everything you can about the area you would like to be successful in as well as other areas. Get on the Internet and read the news, blogs, articles, and eBooks, or go to the library or bookstore. If you haven't  read in a while, just start with a topic you will enjoy learning more about.

2.   Be an active listener

In conversations, be an active listener, especially when you are surrounded by people who have the skills and knowledge you want. As you listen, ask questions and dig deeper about their ideas and you will be on your way to adding a new interest in your life. You can also listen to podcasts or audio books. When you are listening to these, ask yourself whether you agree or disagree with what you're hearing, or whether you would like to learn more about this subject, or whether there is something you don't understand.

3.   It's OK to not know

I used to think I had to be a know-it-all, but I learned that being a know-it-all closed off my learning channels and opportunities. Experts don't know it all. Accepting and admitting that you don't know shows you are self-confident and that you want to learn.

4.   Action

You can read every book on basketball and you can listen to podcasts and watch videos but that will not make you a successful basketball player. To do that, you would have to grab a basketball and go shoot some hoops and learn the basic skills of the sport. Action is required!

5. Teach others

I do this. With whatever I learn, I will find someone who would be interested in the topic and share what I have learned. It's simple; teaching someone reinforces your own learning. Be curious, make learning a priority and ask questions because to achieve success you must do what most people are unwilling to do. We all have different styles of learning. You just need to find the right learning style for you. It could be a combination.

Kinesthetic learners learn and remember information by experimenting and using their sense of touch. Like young children who have to feel something or put it in their mouth. Auditory learners learn and remember information by listening. Listening to music while studying or listening to podcasts. Visual learners learn and remember information with images when they see pictures, symbols, or videos. Which one are you?

Now, we will share with you an exercise to reveal the secret of learning. You will get into a state of relaxation and alertness and turn off the internal chatter. To learn and be more attentive, use this before you drive, teach, learn, and so on. Watch our demo on the website.

Below is the script for you to follow as well as teach others.

1. Pick a spot on the wall that's higher than eye level. Relax your back and jaw.

2. Stare at the spot for about 30 seconds. You should only focus on the spot—tunnel vision.

3. Keep staring at the spot and just expand your vision. At this point you become aware of the things on either side of you. You will begin to see the things on the right and left of you. You may notice the wall on either side or maybe someone sitting in the corner.

4. When you are ready, while you are still staring at the spot, keep expanding the peripheral vision so you can feel the people behind you or the wall behind you.

5. When you have a 360-degree visual, bring your eyes down to eye level.

What's different than before? Do you feel calmer? Are you experiencing change in your concentration? Are you more focused?

Going back to the time when Bhavini looked at me in shock and disbelief and said no to the idea of us writing a book. Well, after a three-minute conversation we embarked on a learning journey that we had not dreamed of, nor had chatted about nor was it on our radar.

Join the You Got This! Tribe.

Share what you will be doing differently, what questions you have, and what we need to know.

www.jalvinicreations.com/yougotthis

Password: change-my-world

NOTES

CHAPTER 8

YOUR COMPELLING FUTURE

*"The big secret in life is that there is no
big secret. Whatever your goal, you can
get there if you're willing to work."*

—Oprah Winfrey

We heard about a young Masaai boy from Kenya called Richard. Richard lived on the edge of the Nairobi National Park. At the age of nine, like most Masaai boys, he was responsible for herding and watching over his family's cows, goats and sheep. One of the downfalls of herding livestock near the National Park is that at night the lions would jump over the fence and feed on the animals. Richard hated the lions. When Richard turned 11, he wanted to come up with a solution to protect his family's livestock. Richard set up a bonfire next to the livestock shed, but the fire helped the lions to see through the fence and they still attacked the animals. The next idea he had was to set up a scarecrow. That scared the lions the first night. The second night the lions realized that the human-like figure was not moving and again they attacked. On another night, Richard decided to walk around the shed with his flashlight.[xxvi]

In this chapter, we will cover how to set goals and ensure you achieve them. Do you set, track and see your goals through?

Humans have always been ambitious. We have built the great pyramids and the Great Wall of China, and we have carved the Panama Canal. It's fair to say humans are all about getting things done. The fundamental key to success is to effectively set goals whether it's taking up a new hobby or dating or learning. In 1968, Dr. Edwin Locke published an article called, *Toward a Theory of Task Motivation and Incentives.* Locke believed that setting clearly identified goals results in superior performance. He proposed five principles of effective goal setting: clarity, challenge, commitment, feedback, and task complexity.[xxvii]

As you recall from Chapter 1, the conscious mind is what we are aware of and it steers and guides us, setting outcomes, and deciding directions. The conscious mind is the goal setter. The unconscious mind is everything that is not conscious. It is a container for different thoughts, feelings, emotions, resources, and possibilities that we are not paying attention to at any one time. Thus, the unconscious mind is the goal getter.

"Setting goals is the first step in turning the invisible into the visible."

—Tony Robbins

A goal is an objective that helps us grow, expand, and push ourselves to transform in ways we would have never imagined. Sometimes that goal may be small like waking up an hour earlier and sometimes it may be bigger like getting a promotion. There are different types of goals and you can categorize them into health, career, relationships, lifestyle and so on. Here is the kicker some people will say goal setting doesn't work. Well, one of the most common reasons that people don't achieve their goals is that their goals aren't compelling or inspiring enough. You need to be excited to jump out of bed every morning to work on achieving your goal. General goals may be difficult to measure and test, making it difficult to determine whether you are making strides toward your goal. Unless your goals are time based, it's very easy for them to be stuck in the hamster wheel where they are never really left behind nor achieved. For example, lots of people want to lose weight because they want to be fit, healthy, and live longer. For whatever reason, they never take the first step or they quit.

Enter S.M.A.R.T goals, which overcome all the pitfalls associated with general goals. You will create and maintain power with S.M.A.R.T goals to give you the maximum possible outcome. S.M.A.R.T stands for Specific, Measurable, Achievable, Relevant and Time based.

Specific

Make your goal specific and positive so it allows you to be clear and laser focused. Being specific allows you to be truly motivated to achieve your goal. To set a specific goal you need to answer the five "W" questions:

- What do I want to accomplish?
- Why is this goal important?
- Who is involved?
- Where is it located?
- Which resources or limits are involved?

For example, "I will get to my optimal weight" is clearer and more specific than "I want to lose weight," which is vague. If a goal is too general, it causes difficulties in developing an action plan.

"Vague goals result in vague results.
Clarity breeds mastery."

—Robin Sharma

Measurable

It is important to track your progress and stay motivated. Measurable goals allow you to set benchmarks that help you to stay focused, re-evaluate when you don't meet them and celebrate when you do. Below are questions you need to answer to assure you have a measurable goal.

- How much?

- How many?
- How will I know when it is accomplished?

For example, "I will lose 20 pounds in increments of 1 pound a week." Your goal must have an aspect that can be measured and evaluated.

"Make measurable progress in reasonable time."

—Jim Rohn

Achievable

Many people fail because they set impossible goals for themselves. Impossible goals push you forward only for a while and at some point, you give up on them. You want to identify goals that are important to you and that you can envision yourself achieving; thus, your goal should be challenging yet achievable with the right steps. For example, "I will accomplish getting to my optimal weight by implementing the 26-week clean-eating habit challenge."

"What you get by achieving your goals is not as important as what you become by achieving your goals."

—Henry David Thoreau

Relevant

You want to ensure that your goal matters, is worthwhile, aligns and is relevant to your overall plan for your life. If your goal is relevant, your answers to the questions below would be yes.

- Does this seem worthwhile?
- Is this the right time?
- Does this match my other goals?
- Am I the right person to reach this goal?

For example, "Weight loss and clean eating are relevant to my other goals of getting healthier and cooking for myself."

"People with goals succeed because
they know where they are going."

—Earl Nightingale

Time Based

A goal must have a target date because that will trigger a sense of urgency and dismiss all forms of procrastination. For a time-based goal, you would answer the following questions:

- When?
- What can I do six months from now?
- What can I do six weeks from now?
- What can I do today?

For example, "I will get to my optimal weight six months from today."

"A goal is a dream with a deadline."

—Napoleon Hill

When setting a goal, you should have a clear outcome in mind so you can achieve the goal. Every feature of S.M.A.R.T should be goal oriented. Here is an example of a formulated S.M.A.R.T statement for weight loss. "On June 30th, 2021, I am celebrating achieving my optimal weight by losing 20 pounds in increments of 1 pound a week by following and implementing the 26-week clean-eating habit challenge and living my best healthy life." Here is an exercise to help you set goals.

Take a piece of paper and write down 10 big-picture goals you would like to accomplish in the next year. Look through your list and ask yourself which goal would have the greatest positive impact on your life and by when? When you go through the 10 goals, you will determine the top 1 or 2 most important general goals you would like to accomplish by the end of the year. You will write the general goal as a S.M.A.R.T goal using the criteria above or you can download the S.M.A.R.T goal template on our website. Next, break the most important goal into smaller benchmarks that you must hit to reach your big goal. Finally, you will create a game plan for your benchmarks that will keep you focused to achieve the big goal.

Richard walked around the shed with his flashlight at night. He had his aha moment the following morning when he observed that the lions had stayed away and none of his livestock was harmed. Richard discovered that lions are scared of moving light. A few weeks later, he came up with an innovative, simple, effective, and low-cost system to scare the predators away. He designed the Lion Lights, which were light bulbs that flickered on and off intermittently tricking the lions into believing that someone was moving around with a flashlight. Richard created and installed the whole system on his own without any training in electronics or engineering. Richard was invited to speak at the TED 2013 Conference in California. Richard's invention has been installed for various neighbours and communities in Kenya and it has saved their livestock.

Join the You Got This! Tribe.

Share what you will be doing differently, what questions you have, and what we need to know.

www.jalvinicreations.com/yougotthis

Password: change-my-world

NOTES

CHAPTER 9

DREAM & CREATE
YOUR FUTURE

*"Vision without action is merely a dream.
Vision with action can change the world."*

—Joel A. Barker

Many years ago, a Chinese farmer was barely able to provide for himself and his family. He was so poor that he had nothing of value but a chicken that unfortunately did not lay any eggs. The farmer grew the basics to feed his family; however, he wanted to grow something that would solve his financial problems and thus did some research on various other crops to grow. One day he set out to the market with his mindset to trade the only chicken he had for bamboo

seeds to plant on his farm. At the market, he came across an old man who was interested in his chicken in exchange for tiny beige-colored seeds. The old man assured him that the seeds would grow into towering bamboo trees that would provide him with all he needed to sustain himself and his family for the rest of his days. The old man also mentioned he would need to be patient and use the power of visualization. The following day, the farmer got up early to prepare the land to plant his seeds. By mid-day, he was done. After planting the seeds, he spent his days carrying water from the river to where he had planted the seeds and watered them. He continued with this process for weeks, then months. Some days it would rain pitter-patter, pitter-patter, pitter-patter. The first year, all his other crops grew fine; however, the bamboo seeds did not grow. Not even a peep. No shoots, no glimpses of this mythical Chinese bamboo anywhere. The farmer stuck at it and knew something good was going to happen. During the second year, the farmer continued to water the seeds and made sure he weeded the land as well. Eventually people started laughing and mocking him and told him to give up as it had been three years, and nothing was happening on the land. The farmer ignored them and still watered his seeds. Four years went by and there was still no sign of a bamboo tree, or any life from the ground where he had planted the seeds years ago. The farmer called a friend who had had experience in growing this magical Chinese bamboo. His friend reassured him that it was only a matter of time now and if he were to give up, he would lose everything and have to start all over again. "Please stick with it," his friend begged, "you have spent all this time tending the land. If you give up now, you will lose everything and have to start all over again. I promise you that, one day, those Chinese bamboo trees will grow. Make sure you continue your visualization exercise." Well, the fourth year went by and still nothing. One day the town's people came rushing to the farmer as they heard him screaming!

In this chapter, you will begin your journey to dream and create your future. Do you want to turn your life around, experience living your life and be ready to take action on your biggest dreams?

Anyone in the commercial TV, web video, or film production industry knows that they need to create a storyboard to map out their films before shooting the screens. The storyboard also helps to zoom in and focus on the star (that's you!).

One of the simplest tools to help you visualize your dreams and goals is a vision board. Vision boards are tangible, fun, and powerful ways to get what you want in your life! Research shows that in the caveman era, cave paintings were painted in advance of a hunt. For instance, the artist would visualize the experience of hunting and paint it on the wall.[xxviii] Many people have been using vision boards for years for various reasons (wedding planning, buying a new car, weight loss goals, and so on). Back in 1997, Jim Carrey was on the Oprah Winfrey show and he talked about visualization.

In 1987, Jim Carrey was virtually broke and really wanted to be in the entertainment industry. Every single night, he would park his car on the famous Mulholland Drive in Los Angeles, USA and visualize having directors interested in him and people he respected saying, "I like your work." Jim Carrey wrote himself a cheque for $10 million. He dated the cheque for Thanksgiving 1995 and in the memo section, wrote "For acting services rendered." He stuck that cheque in his wallet and carried it with him for years. Just before Thanksgiving 1995, Jim Carrey learned that he would be making $10 million for his role in the movie *Dumb and Dumber*. Other famous people like Oprah Winfrey, Steve Harvey, Lilly Singh, Ellen DeGeneres, John Assaraf and many more use vision boards to bring their dreams to reality. In 2006, the book and movie, *The Secret* made vision boards a popular activity.[xxix]

Back in Chapter 1, we explored what the unconscious mind is set up to provide and do for us. One thing it does is create, use, and respond to symbols. The images you embed in your mind instantly set up an attraction force that determines the results in your life. We also looked at the conscious mind being the goal setter whereas the unconscious mind is the goal getter!

You know when you buy or are thinking of buying something, say, a new red car and suddenly you see red cars appear everywhere? That's because you have focused your attention on something specific and are unconsciously scanning the world for items that match it. It's not that those cars were never there, it's just that you never noticed them before right now. Here's the science behind it. There is a part of the brain that arouses and motivates you. This part is called the reticular activating system (RAS). The RAS is the little bundle of cells situated at the core of the brain stem between the medulla and the midbrain. The RAS serves as the filter for what enters your conscious and unconscious mind. Without our RAS, we would be overwhelmed by information overload. The capacity of our conscious mind is limited, while the unconscious mind is unlimited. Also, our beliefs and values guide what the RAS focuses upon. Just like the red cars, the principle applies to other things in our lives like happiness, health, and success. When you aren't focusing on them, they disappear into your unconscious mind.

"Mind your thoughts; they become your words.
Mind your words; they become your actions.
Mind your actions; they become your habits.
Mind your habits; they become your destiny."

—Socrates & Aristotle

Let's explore the ways that the vision board helps you reach your goals.

1. Makes you focus on what's important to you.

Whether you combine a personal vision board with a professional one or keep them separate, thinking about what you want in life forces you to prioritize what's important. Do you want to go back to school? Buy your first house? Move to a warmer climate? Putting up a photo of the school you'd like to attend, or a photo of your dream location will inspire you to work harder. You alone can make that dream happen and you will make better decisions based on that desire.

2. Visualization stimulates the creative side of your brain.

Placing your vision board in sight serves as a daily reminder of what you want to achieve. Placing your vision board by your nightstand helps stimulate your unconscious mind before you go to bed, which makes you motivated upon waking. With your creativity soaring, keep a notebook handy to jot down any ideas you have. Consistent visualization trains your mind, body and spirit to manifest your desires.

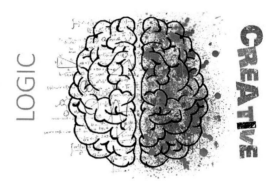

3. Focusing on goals makes you recognize new resources and opportunities.

Visualizing whatever your primary goal is will motivate you to work toward that goal and you will also notice new opportunities and resources which can lead you to reaching your goal. These resources may have always been present and now that you are focused on your goal, you will see them in a new light to help you reach that intended goal.

4. Break out of your comfort zone by stating a big, scary goal.
Are you stuck in a rut because you're afraid to break out of your comfort zone? Acknowledging big goals, as scary and outrageous as they may be, will help you step out and take new challenges, all in the name of reaching that scary goal.

"Be your own magician and change your world!"

—Tejal and Bhavini Solanki

5. Seeing a big goal forces you out of the daydream and into action.
Nothing happens without some action on your part. Vision boards are not magic tricks, they are a tool that spurs us into action because we finally know what we want out of life. Visualize your ideal life then approach each day with action steps which will lead you toward that ideal life.

Vision boards can be made any time of the year! Waiting for the New Year or your birthday is an option; however, you can create a vision board today.

Before you create a vision board, you want to look back on the past year or six months and be grateful for what life has brought to you. Every situation, positive or negative, is a teaching moment, so be grateful. Recognize and accept your progress and accomplishments thus far. (Go ahead and treat yourself!). Look at all the things that no longer serve a purpose in your life and let go, for instance old ideas, habits, and limiting beliefs. Letting go will open up space within yourself to receive new ideas and opportunities right now and onward. Being open and authentic will enable you to ask questions and seek guidance toward your new goals. As you move forward, you want to share what you have learned. As discussed in Chapter 7, sharing what you learn increases the power to change your life and you will inspire others.

*"Your vision will become clear only when
you can look into your own heart. Who looks
outside dreams; who looks inside awakes."*

—Carl Jung

Let's create the vision board! Here are our simple steps for creating an empowering vision board.

1.   Plan out your board.

Start with our guided visualization available on our website. After the guided visualization, write down any words, colors, symbols, and so on that popped up. You will also be able to journal about all the things you want to be, do, or have in various areas of your life. Imagine your ideal relationship, career, body, and so on. Also think about whether you want one board or multiple boards for different areas of your life.

2. Gather your materials.

Some people find it fun to flip through magazines and cut out images and words that call out to them and spark positive emotions. You would need a variety of old magazines or you could find images on the Internet that are representative of what you DO WANT. Do you really want to earn the sporty BMW convertible, or do you want the freedom and carefree life the photo symbolizes? If you are creating a handmade vision board you will need a poster board, scissors, magazines, glue or tape. If you do not plan to create a handmade vision board, consider creating a digital version with MS PowerPoint or Google Slides or Pinterest.

3. Create your vision board.

Less is more. Keep your vision board simple and literal. Make sure there is space between the images and that the images are entirely visible.

4. Display it.

Once you have created your vision board, place it in an area that you see every day. Remember

to sit with it at least once a day for 10 minutes to reflect and for it to be a source of motivation to keep working toward your goals and to accomplish them. You will also be able to visit the feelings of happiness and gratitude of eventually having those desires in your life. The last thing you want is for your vision board to become a piece of furniture! You can take a picture of your handmade vision board and put it as a wallpaper on your phone or computer. If it's digital, save it as an image screenshot and have it on your screensaver. You can also print it out and place it in an area where you will look at it every day.

5.   Spring into action.

Vision boards are not mystical or magical. Just because you put photos together and post the board in your office or bedroom doesn't mean things will start magically appearing. Even if you want to win the lottery, you still need to take the action to buy the ticket, right? The same is true for vision boards.

6.   Let the universe do its thing.

Hold the images on your vision board in your awareness and begin to acknowledge and accept the opportunities as they present themselves to make your dreams a reality. Vision boards do not need to be perfect and can be flexible and fluid as everyone's vision board is unique. Vision boards can be made every 6 to 12 months to be sure they are present, inspiring, and up to date with your values and priorities.

Remember the Chinese farmer who planted the bamboo tree seeds? In the fifth year, the town's people came rushing to the farmer as they heard him screaming! Finally, there were green sprouts bursting out of the ground. In the second week, the small shoots grew to the size

 of a small plant. Six weeks later the Chinese bamboo had grown 90 feet high. After five excruciating years of hard work and doubt, the farmer's patience, visualization, and perseverance had paid off.

Join the You Got This! Tribe.

Share what you will be doing differently, what questions you have, and what we need to know.

www.jalvinicreations.com/yougotthis

Password: change-my-world

NOTES

CHAPTER 10

TRIBE: FINDING THE RIGHT PEOPLE FOR YOU

"Find a group of people who challenge and inspire you, spend a lot of time with them, and it will change your life."

—Amy Poehler

We have an uncle who still lives in Nairobi, Kenya. He wears dark sunglasses and always has to put medication in his eyes. Our uncle had a medication reaction, which caused his tear duct glands to dry out. For years he has been seeing an ophthalmologist almost every week to once a month. As we were writing this book, we received news that our uncle's eyesight was deteriorating at an alarming rate. His ophthalmologist in Nairobi referred him to an eye specialist in India for an urgent cornea transplant which would save him from losing his sight. This transplant was going to cost thousands of dollars and is not covered by the Ministry of Health or by private insurance.

With this in mind, in this chapter we will look at finding the right people for you. Do you feel alone, have no one to talk to, and face difficulties by yourself? In this fast-paced life, you can find yourself feeling like an island even though you are surrounded by family, friends, coworkers or groups, and nobody knows enough about how to help you to reach your success. Most times our friends and family are too close to us emotionally to give unbiased advice or opinions due to their own personal gain or genuinely not wanting to hurt you, or they lack the knowledge about what you are dealing with. Thinking outside the box and finding the right people for you (tribe),will help you get through whatever it is, whether it's for your personal or professional success.

A tribe is "your people" that you choose to be with because you have an important connection on a higher level and they are part of some aspect of your core identity. Having a sense of belonging and being understood is what a tribe can do for you. A community is a group of people you share something in common with and may be considerably less personal. A tribe is where you choose who is in your circle and a community is where you are permanently connected through association. There is a time and place for both.

In 1961, research conducted on a community of people in Roseto, Pennsylvania revealed evidence of how tribes benefit their members both physically and mentally. The Roseto community had half the risk of death by heart attack and not because of genetics or eating or drinking habits. The community would get together and would eat Italian sausage and meatballs fried in lard and would drink as much wine as they could drink. They had no crime and no one on welfare. The members were dying of old age or illnesses contracted from gases and dust from the slate quarries that they worked in.

The research concluded that love, intimacy, and being part of the tribe protected the community members' health. While the people of Roseto meet the definition of a community, they are also a tribe because they choose to spend time together and participate together in activities.[xxx]

If you recall, in Chapter 3, we looked at the sneaky villains with whom you are spending most of your time and whether they were energy drainers or energy chargers. You want to surround yourself with energy chargers and people who have that same mindset. You want to start creating or joining a new tribe. Finding the right people for you means stepping out of your comfort zone and doing things that are unfamiliar and maybe a little stressful, with the right amount of pressure to push you forward. In Chapter 7, we talked about successful people who are constantly learning and who will seek and find people who know what they are talking about and will learn from them.

Tribes are different, relevant, and magical. Seth Godin describes a tribe as, "group of people connected to one another, connected to a leader, and connected to an idea. For millions of years, human beings have been part of one tribe or another. A group needs only two things to be a tribe—a shared interest and a way to communicate."[xxxi] Examples of tribes are friends, veterans group, discussion groups, seminar classes, pottery classes, book clubs, spiritual groups, hypnosis groups, coaching groups. A community is generally based, for example, on the neighbourhood you live in, the religious organization you were raised in, life within a pond, social status, and many more identities. We have been members of tribes and leaders of communities and have seen the power of tribe first hand. Here are some benefits tribes provide to members.

Affinity

Defined as a spontaneous or natural liking for someone. Tribes offer non-blood-tie relationships that have similar characteristics to kinships. This is where friends are like family.

Intimacy

Members become very close and are able to share the good, the bad and the ugly without judgment.

Faith and Belief

Tribes have a lot of faith and a solid belief that they have each other's back and that they can accomplish anything together.

Authenticity

This is where tribe members hold space for each other with no judgments. Imperfections and vulnerability are welcomed and encouraged.

Availability

Someone will be available and be there when you need them, whether it is to answer a question, be a sounding board, or be the out of the box solution.

Dependability and Support

Tribe members will check in on each other and make sure no one is left behind. Tribe members ask for help when they need it.

There are some traits the tribe members need to possess to become valued and accepted.

1. **Know thyself. Be thyself.** You need to be authentic, be self-aware and be connected with what is going on within you.
2. **Get over yourself.** The power of tribes comes from the contributions of all members.
3. **We are not perfect.** People do mess up and that's okay! Yay Human! Tribe members find a solution and get to the root cause and put preventive measures in place. You want to build up the people around you instead of breaking them down.
4. **Give as much as, if not more than, you receive.** Be prepared to contribute more than you get. The energy of give and take will go back and forth like the infinity sign.

You can be brave and start a group. You never know where it might lead to and what connections you might make. Heck, finding a tribe requires effort, authenticity, and confidence. Here's an exercise to get you started and get you to move forward, as there is a tribe waiting for you.

1.   Learn about yourself/make a list

Make a list of the things you have and are really enjoying and another list of the things you feel are missing from your life. Do you love dancing salsa but don't have a dancing partner? Do you like to go on hikes, but feel as though none of your friends ever want to go with you? Once you are aware of what you are looking for, you will be able to look for tribes/groups of people that will fill that gap.

2. Get out of your comfort zone

Remember, a vision with no action is a dream. You have to step out of your comfort zone and sign up for a salsa class, surfing lessons, or improv class because you never know who you will meet. You will also learn a lot about yourself and what types of people you want to make space for in your life. One of the ways to get started is to look into meetups and clubs. There are thousands of meetups dedicated to yoga, salsa dancing, hiking, video games, coin collecting, filmmaking, wine tasting, and so many more.

Remember, our uncle who needed the cornea transplant that was not covered by the Ministry of Health or private insurance? Well, our tribe members in Kenya got together and established a fundraising committee. The message reached far and wide across the world to various communities. People donated to the cause whether they knew him or not. The fundraising efforts exceeded the targeted amount. Our uncle and family were overwhelmed and grateful to the tribe and communities that came together in his dire need to assist him.

Join the You Got This! Tribe.
Share what you will be doing differently, what questions you have, and what we need to know.
www.jalvinicreations.com/yougotthis
Password: change-my-world

NOTES

CONCLUSION

BRING IT TO LIFE

"The most effective way to do it, is to do it."

—Amelia Earhart

There you have it! It's easy, right? We know there are aspects of this book that will be challenging; however, you have a new outlook and a deeper understanding of how to unleash your strength, power, and potential to change your world. We hope you've discovered new things about yourself! Remember, the magic happens outside your comfort zone with a little or a lot of discomfort and pressure. Keep track of your progress through your small wins and learnings from various situations you encounter in life. Keep in mind that through the various stages of life you will continue to discover your path, transform yourself and empower your life to reach your potential both personally and professionally. Any change you make in life will be difficult in the beginning, messy in the middle, and absolutely worth it in the end. Now go out there and make it happen! You Got This!

For additional tools, templates, and recommendations visit
www.jalvinicreations.com/yougotthis
Password: change-my-world

ACKNOWLEDGEMENTS

"Every book, every volume you see here, has a soul. The soul of the person who wrote it and of those who read it and lived and dreamed with it. Every time a book changes hands, every time someone runs his eyes down its pages, its spirit grows and strengthens."

—Carlos Ruiz Zafón, *The Shadow of the Wind*

Thank you for investing your time and energy with us. Embrace your fear as fuel because you can do whatever you set your mind to. We look forward to hearing from you! There are no words to express our gratitude to the special people in our lives who have supported us through the process, particularly our parents Dhirendra and Kalpana Solanki, our friend Raza Aziz, Sheila Masters, our friend and mentor, and our uncle and aunt, Hiten and Neeta Nathoo. We would also like to thank everyone who donated to our book campaign. As always, thank you to our friends and family for their love and support.

RESOURCES
Want More?
Here are some resources to help!

For additional tools, templates, and recommendations visit
www.jalvinicreations.com/yougotthis
Password: change-my-world

Follow us on Facebook at
www.facebook.com/jalvinicreations

Want personal help to move from being stuck and lost to reclaiming your strength and power?
Book a FREE 30-minute consult with us
www.jalvinicreations.com

REFERENCES

i   https://beyondpenguins.ehe.osu.edu/issue/icebergs-and-glaciers/all-about-icebergs

ii   https://myhealth.alberta.ca/Health/Pages/conditions.aspx?hwid=sta123093&

iii   https://www.simplypsychology.org/unconscious-mind.html

iv   https://www.simplypsychology.org/carl-jung.html

v   https://www.betterhelp.com/advice/psychologists/how-milton-erickson-revolutionized-modern-therapy/

vi   https://www.consciouslifestylemag.com/subconscious-mind-power/

vii   https://www.ahajournals.org/doi/full/10.1161/01.cir.101.17.2034

viii   https://openaccesspub.org/ijpr/article/999

ix   https://www.deepakchopra.com/blog/article/4701

x   https://positivepsychology.com/negative-emotions/

xi   https://www.takingcharge.csh.umn.edu/how-do-thoughts-and-emotions-affect-health

xii   https://onlinelibrary.wiley.com/doi/10.1002/cne.920180503

xiii   https://www.ted.com/talks/amy_cuddy_your_body_language_may_shape_who_you_are/up-next

xiv   https://www.ncbi.nlm.nih.gov/pmc/articles/PMC3096184/

xv https://www150.statcan.gc.ca/n1/pub/82-003-x/2017009/article/54857-eng.htm

xvi http://sleepeducation.org/news/2013/08/01/sleep-and-caffeine

xvii https://www.ncbi.nlm.nih.gov/pmc/articles/PMC5438379/

xviii https://www.ncbi.nlm.nih.gov/pmc/articles/PMC3679190/

xix https://www.webmd.com/fitness-exercise/news/20120824/30-minutes-daily-exercise-shed-pounds

xx https://www.health.harvard.edu/newsletter_article/a-prescription-for-better-health-go-alfresco

xxi https://health.clevelandclinic.org/3-reasons-adult-coloring-can-actually-relax-brain/

xxii Lewis, B. and Pucelik, R., 2012. Magic Of NLP Demystified. 2nd ed. Bancyfelin: Crown House, pp.39-47.

xxiii https://www.psychologytoday.com/us/blog/between-cultures/201906/are-negative-emotions-universally-bad-our-health

xxiv https://www.psychologytoday.com/ca/blog/curious/201003/science-shows-you-can-die-boredom-literally

xxv https://faculty.washington.edu/chudler/plast.html

xxvi https://www.ted.com/talks/richard_turere_my_invention_that_made_peace_with_lions/up-next?language=en

xxvii http://garfield.library.upenn.edu/classics1982/A1982NJ34100001.pdf

xxviii https://www.theguardian.com/science/2012/mar/11/cave-painting-symbols-language-evolution

xxix https://www.thesecret.tv/products/the-secret-book/

xxx https://www.ncbi.nlm.nih.gov/pmc/articles/PMC2376462/pdf/tacca00088-0118.pdf

xxxi https://seths.blog/wp-content/uploads/2008/11/TribesQA2.pdf